HAIR TODAY, BRAIDS TOMORROW

BRAIDS, PONYTAILS & BUNS FOR YOUNG GIRLS

BEGINNERS GUIDE TO ALL THINGS HAIR

SHELBY WELBORN

TABLE OF CONTENT

BOOK DESCRIPTION

Every morning, as the sun stretches its golden fingers across the sky, a world of possibilities awakens. For young girls, each day is a canvas waiting to be painted with adventures, dreams, and the delightful surprises that life has in store. And what better way to start this daily journey than by adorning oneself with a crown of creative, expressive, and charming hairstyles?

In the world of childhood, where imagination reigns supreme, we believe that hair can be more than just strands woven together; it can be a canvas for self-expression, a source of bonding, and a doorway to endless fun. This is the essence of "Cool Braids, Buns & Ponytails for Girls – A Comprehensive Guide to Creative Casual and Formal Hair Styling for Girls."

PURPOSE UNVEILED

This book is more than just a collection of hairstyles; it's a guidebook designed to be your companion on a magical journey through the world of hair styling. Our purpose is simple yet profound: to provide young girls and their parents or caregivers with a comprehensive, easy-to-follow resource that unlocks the secrets of creative hair styling.

Whether you're a parent looking to create dazzling hairdos for your little one, a big sister wanting to bond over braids and buns, or a young girl eager to explore the world of hair design, this book is for you. From the simplest of ponytails to intricate braids fit for royalty, we've crafted this guide with love, passion, and the understanding that every girl is unique and deserves to shine in her own way.

WHY WE WROTE THIS BOOK

Have you ever faced the morning rush, struggling to decide on the perfect hairstyle for school or a special occasion? Have you wished for a go-to resource that not only provides step-by-step instructions but also encourages creativity and self-expression through hair styling? We understand those dilemmas, and that's why we wrote this book.

We know that every parent and caregiver want the best for their child, and every young girl wants to feel confident and fabulous. Yet, the world of hair styling can seem daunting with its myriad of techniques, tools, and products. We're here to simplify it all, to break down the barriers, and to guide you on a journey where hair styling becomes not just a daily chore but a delightful art.

WHAT LIES AHEAD

In the chapters that follow, we will introduce you to the essential tools and supplies you need to embark on this exciting adventure. We'll unravel the mysteries of basic techniques, giving you the foundation to create stunning braids, buns, and ponytails. We'll explore a wide array of creative styles suitable for casual outings and formal events. And, as an extra treat, we'll introduce you to the world of natural herbal hair and scalp products that you can make with your daughter, nurturing both her hair and your bond.

So, let's dive in together, into the world of hair styling where creativity knows no bounds. Let's transform mornings into moments of joy, where the act of styling becomes an act of love and celebration. Welcome to "HAIR TODAY, BRAIDS TOMORROW" – where dreams are woven into every strand.

Are you ready to embark on this beautiful journey with us?

INTRODUCTION TO HAIR STYLING

Welcome to the exciting world of hair styling! This chapter serves as your gateway to the art of creative hair design, whether you're a parent, caregiver, or an adventurous young girl eager to explore the possibilities that hair can offer. Before we dive into the intricacies of braids, buns, and ponytails, let's lay the foundation for your hair styling journey.

THE MAGIC OF HAIR

Hair is a wondrous thing. It's not just a collection of strands that grow from our scalps; it's a versatile medium for expression and creativity. Every strand holds the potential to become a work of art. Hair is like nature's paintbrush, and with it, we can craft masterpieces that reflect our unique personalities, moods, and styles.

WHY HAIR STYLING MATTERS

The act of styling hair goes far beyond aesthetics. It's a powerful means of self-expression, boosting confidence and providing a sense of individuality. For young girls, a well-styled mane can be a source of pride, helping them feel like the confident, creative individuals they are. For parents and caregivers, it's a chance to bond with their children, share moments of connection, and build lasting memories.

WHY BRAIDING MATTERS

I set out on a quest ten years ago to research the global hair braiding customs. Why? Because I was curious as to why, despite the fact that hair braiding, in all of its forms, has long been a common styling method throughout cultures, people often tended to see African-styled braiding negatively.

I have always cherished braids, both making and wearing them. I consider hair braiding to be an art form, thus I have never understood (and still don't understand) why some people find it offensive. Therefore, I wanted to assist others in understanding the beauty and relevance of hair braiding, not just for those of African origin but for all people. I genuinely wanted others to understand the importance of hair braiding as a human practice.

In addition, most of my college classmates and many other black women I knew at the time I wrote my Watson project proposal had never been taught how to braid and, in many cases, had no actual need or desire to learn since, for the most part, they wore their hair straight. This meant that the long-standing black cultural tradition of elaborate braiding was no longer being passed down from mothers to daughters.

Thankfully, things were slowly but surely beginning to shift back toward the natural state of women. As a result, braids—which for a very long time had only been used to maintain the hair of young girls—started to be regarded as a suitable stylistic option once more. However, many mothers still did not learn how to braid themselves or, for that matter, educate their daughters.

The "going natural" trend has evolved into a movement ten years later, and with the Natural Hair Movement now in full swing, I think the skill of braiding has never been more crucial.

The following are some reasons why I believe braiding is important (and why you should learn it and teach your children to do it, too), even though I don't anticipate anyone being as passionate about braids as I am:

Daily management and maintenance are made easier by braiding shrinkage. If you have shrinking in your hair, braiding can help stretch it.

If your hair is thick, braiding it into sections can make the washing, conditioning, and moisturizing processes simpler.

Oiling your scalp is simpler when your hair is braided.

Once your hair is braided, you need to spend less time on it every day.

Before you go to sleep at night, even merely plaiting your hair can make all the difference between having a manageable head of hair and having to spend hours the next day detangling your matted locks.

A braid-out, also known as a heat-free crimp, can be made by braiding.

THE IMPORTANCE OF SELF EXPRESSION AND CREATIVITY THROUGH HAIR.

Without using words, one can express themselves through their hair in a way that defies social conventions or pays homage to their culture.

One of a person's most distinguishing physical characteristics, whether it is coloured, cropped, or curled, is their hair. Hair has long been a key component of fashion, self-expression, and how someone is seen in society. You can alter your personality by changing your hairstyle, hair color, or haircut. They outline your identity and your aspirations.

Because it's the first thing that people see and because I believe that hair and fashion go hand in hand, "[my hair] is something I feel will help represent my identity as well as fashion, " It means a lot to me. I've come to truly enjoy it over the years and know that, unlike most other aspects of my life, it is something that I can manage. I suppose that in that regard, hair is quite important to me.

Many kids' hairstyles were chosen by a caregiver as they grew up. While there could have been a choice of styles, teenagers often have greater freedom because they are not subject to the expectations that are placed on people of other ages.

Additionally, hair serves as a creative outlet. It might develop into a social activity or just a way to decompress from daily life.

Let's delve deeper into the significance of these elements:

THE POWER OF SELF-EXPRESSION:

Individuality and Identity: Hair styling allows individuals, especially young girls, to express their unique personalities and identity. It's a form of non-verbal communication that says, "This is who I am, and I'm proud of it." Whether it's a bold, adventurous look or a simple, elegant style, how we

choose to style our hair can convey our character and preferences.

Boosting Self-Confidence: When we feel good about our appearance, our self-esteem soars. A well-styled mane can instill a sense of confidence and empowerment. For young girls, especially during crucial developmental years, this boost in confidence can have a profound impact on their self-worth.

Emotional Expression: Hair styling can be a means of emotional expression. Different hairstyles can reflect various moods and emotions. A fun, playful hairstyle might represent joy and enthusiasm, while a more subdued style might indicate a calm and composed demeanor.

Adaptation and Exploration: Hair is a versatile medium that allows us to adapt to different situations and explore various looks. It's like having a wardrobe for your head. You can choose styles that suit a casual day at school, a formal event, or a themed party, showcasing your adaptability and creativity.

✱ THE ART OF CREATIVITY:

Endless Possibilities: Hair styling is an art form with limitless possibilities. From intricate braids to whimsical updos, the only limit is your imagination. It's a space where you can push boundaries and experiment with colors, accessories, and textures.

Personal Expression: Just as painters have a canvas and colors, hair stylists have hair as their medium. Each style you create is a unique masterpiece, reflecting your creativity and artistic vision. It's an opportunity to express your personal style and artistic flair.

Learning and Growth: Creativity thrives on learning and growth. With each new style you attempt, you acquire new skills and insights. You may discover innovative ways to combine techniques, adapt trends, or even invent your own signature styles.

Connection and Bonding: Creativity also fosters connection. When parents, caregivers, or friends come together to experiment with hair styling, it's a bonding experience. It's a time to share ideas, collaborate, and create something beautiful together.

Confidence in Experimentation: Encouraging creativity through hair styling promotes a willingness to experiment and take risks in other aspects of life. It teaches us that it's okay to try new things, make mistakes, and learn from them—an invaluable life skill.

In essence, self-expression and creativity through hair styling go hand in hand. It's about embracing the freedom to be yourself, communicate your uniqueness, and explore the boundless world of artistic expression through hair. Whether you're crafting a simple ponytail or a complex braided masterpiece, each creation is a testament to your individuality and creativity. So, embrace the art of hair styling as a canvas for self-expression and let your creativity flow.

BENEFITS OF LEARNING VARIOUS BRAIDING TECHNIQUES.

WHAT IS A BRAID?

A braid (or plait) is a flat, three-stranded construction that is made by weaving together one or more strands of material, such as wire, fabric, or hair, to create a pattern. The braid is often long and narrow, with each strand serving the same purpose in zigzagging through the bulk of the other strands that are overlapping it.

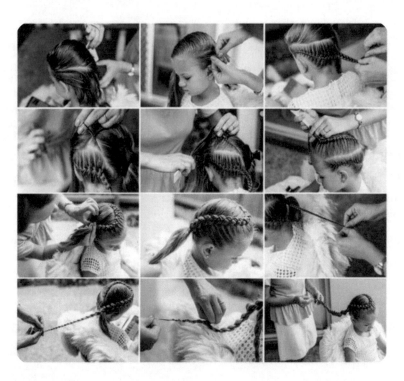

Numerous applications for braiding have been known for thousands of years. Hair braiding was a sign of cultural significance, style, tribal identification, and cultural values among African tribes. A person's community, age, money, marital status, social position, religion, and authority could all be inferred from the many braiding patterns in their hairstyles. One of the main tribes that embraced braiding as a means of expression was the Zulu, followed by the Massai.

Due to their simplicity of upkeep, cornrows (also known as canerows) were frequently preferred. In order to produce cornrows, the hair must be braided very closely to the scalp in an upward, underhanded motion to create a continuous, raised row. The majority of the time, they grow in straight rows from the hairline toward the nape. They can also be shaped in highly specific curvilinear or geometric patterns, though.

In paintings that date back as early as 3000 B.C., women with cornrows have been portrayed. Currently, this stylistic custom is still widely used throughout Africa.

Over time, cornrowing (and hair braiding) experienced a fashionable revival and served as the basis for numerous widely used hair extension methods. The technique of braiding has many applications and will never lose its value.

Hair braiding and cornrowing will provide the fundamental framework for a range of hair styles, and using hair extensions is now more common than ever.

The foundation for connecting wefts, wigs, hair extensions, and latch hook/crochet hair is created by braids.

Braids are excellent for preventive styles when someone wants to keep their hair moisturized and stop shedding while letting their natural hair grow out.

Braids are a fantastic way to express yourself.

ESSENTIAL TOOLS AND SUPPLIES

INTRODUCTION TO HAIRBRUSHES, COMBS, ELASTICS, AND HAIRPINS

B efore diving into the exciting world of hairstyling, it's essential to become familiar with the tools of the trade. Just like a painter relies on brushes and canvases, a hairstylist relies on specific tools to create beautiful hairdos. In this chapter, we'll introduce you to the most common tools you'll need to craft cool braids, buns, and ponytails for girls.

Hair combs work wonders for separating and detangling hair. Wide-toothed combs work best for detangling damp hair, while fine-toothed combs are good for dividing hair into exact sections. However, hair brushes work wonders for straightening and styling hair.

Each one is appropriate for a certain hair type and style and is available in a variety of shapes, sizes, and bristle types.

❋ HAIRBRUSHES:

Hairbrushes come in various shapes, sizes, and materials. They serve multiple purposes, including detangling, smoothing, and adding volume to hair. Here are some common types:

Paddle Brush: Known for its large, flat surface, it's great for detangling and straightening long hair.

Round Brush: Ideal for creating volume and bouncy curls, it's often used during blow-drying.

Vent Brush: Designed for faster drying, it allows air to circulate through the brush, reducing drying time.

Detangling Brush: Perfect for gently removing knots and tangles without causing damage.

When choosing a hairbrush, consider your hair type and the style you want to achieve. The right brush can make a significant difference in the outcome of your hairstyle.

✳ COMBS:

Combs are excellent for precision styling and parting hair. Here are a few types of combs commonly used in hairstyling:

Wide-Tooth Comb: Great for detangling wet hair and distributing conditioner evenly.

Tail Comb: Features a fine, pointed end for creating precise parts and sections.

Rat-Tail Comb: Similar to a tail comb but has a longer, thinner point for intricate styling.

Teasing Comb: Designed with short, close-set teeth for creating volume and teasing hair.

Combs are versatile tools that can help you achieve clean lines and part your hair neatly when creating various hairstyles

✱ ELASTICS:

Hair elastics, also known as hair ties or hair bands, are essential for securing hairstyles like ponytails and braids. They come in different sizes and materials, including fabric-covered elastics, rubber bands, and scrunchies. When choosing elastics, consider the thickness and length of the hair you'll be styling. Thicker hair may require larger or stronger elastics to hold the style securely.

❈ HAIRPINS:

Hairpins, also called bobby pins or hair clips, are small but mighty tools in hairstyling. They come in various lengths and colors to match your hair. Hairpins are used to secure loose strands, pin up sections of hair, or create intricate updos. Learning how to use them effectively is a valuable skill in hairstyling.

HOW TO CHOOSE THE RIGHT PRODUCTS FOR YOUR HAIR TYPE?

Beautiful hair. Every woman dreams of that. Therefore, you should take maximum care of your hair. This means not only visiting your hairdresser regularly, but also using the right cosmetics such as shampoo, conditioner, mask, oils and more. But which hair products are the right ones? Choosing the right hair care cosmetics is not easy due to the wide range of products. What about that? Firstly, it is important to determine your hair type correctly, only then you can choose the right products for your hair.

HOW TO KNOW WHAT TYPE OF HAIR YOU HAVE?

Knowing your hair type is crucial for selecting the haircare products that will work best for you when it comes to taking care of your hair. In fact, employing the wrong products could be the root of many of your top hair concerns or issues. Knowing your hair type will help you find the right balance for your hair and put an end to bad hair days once and for all.

1. STRAIGHT HAIR:

Straight hair is naturally smooth and lacks significant curl or wave. It tends to be fine and can become oily quickly. For straight hair, consider the following products:

Shampoo: Look for a lightweight, clarifying shampoo that removes excess oil without weighing down your hair.

Conditioner: Use a light conditioner on the ends of your hair to prevent dryness without making it greasy.

Styling Products: Opt for volumizing mousses or sprays to add body and texture to straight hair.

2. WAVY HAIR:

Wavy hair has gentle waves or curls that can vary in intensity. It benefits from products that enhance and define its natural texture:

Shampoo: Choose a hydrating shampoo to maintain moisture and prevent frizz.

Conditioner: Use a conditioner that provides moisture and helps define waves without weighing them down.

Styling Products: Consider curl-enhancing creams or mousse to define and control waves.

3. CURLY HAIR:

Curly hair ranges from loose curls to tight coils and tends to be prone to frizz and dryness. Proper products can help manage and nourish curly hair:

Shampoo: Use a sulfate-free, hydrating shampoo to preserve natural oils and prevent excessive drying.

Conditioner: Opt for a rich, moisturizing conditioner to keep curls soft and frizz-free.

Styling Products: Invest in curl-defining gels, creams, or serums to enhance and maintain curl patterns.

4. COILY OR KINKY HAIR:

Coily and kinky hair has tight, spiral-shaped curls and is naturally dry. It requires products that provide intense moisture and definition:

Shampoo: Choose a sulfate-free, moisturizing shampoo to retain natural oils and prevent dryness.

Deep Conditioner: Regularly use a deep conditioner or hair mask to replenish moisture and maintain elasticity.

Styling Products: Use leave-in conditioners, curl-defining creams, or oils to keep coily hair well-hydrated and defined.

5. FINE HAIR:

Fine hair strands are thin in diameter and can lack volume. The right products can add body and prevent flatness:

Volumizing Shampoo: Use a shampoo formulated to add volume and texture.

Lightweight Conditioner: Select a conditioner that won't weigh down fine hair.

Root Lift Products: Consider root-lifting sprays or mousses to boost volume at the roots.

6. THICK OR COARSE HAIR:

Thick or coarse hair strands are larger in diameter and can be challenging to manage. Products that provide moisture and control are beneficial:

Hydrating Shampoo: Look for a moisturizing shampoo to prevent dryness and frizz.

Rich Conditioner: Use a deep conditioner or hair mask to keep thick hair well-nourished and manageable.

Anti-Frizz Products: Consider anti-frizz serums or creams to control unruly hair.

A COMPREHENSIVE GUIDE TO THE DIFFERENT TYPES OF BRAIDS

The art of braiding is ancient, but these styles have never gone out of trend!

Remember the times you wore a straightforward three-strand braid to class? Now, each person gets their own unique braid! If you're confused by the numerous styles of braids, from French braids to braid twists, let us make things simpler for you. You can select a braid for every occasion, whether it be a wedding, business meeting, workout, or date. Your hair is protected from injury with braids, which are a protective hairstyle. Additionally, braided hairstyles might come in handy on days when you haven't washed your hair but suddenly need to leave for somewhere.

And you can wear it with virtually any other hairdo, including twists, ponytails, updos, and free-flowing hair. In addition, there is a braid to suit every mood, from clean to unkempt to everything in between. Braids are really adaptable in this way! Here is a comprehensive reference to all the many braid styles, how to braid hair, and how you may try them all out to help you find your way through this vast world of braiding. Read on to learn more.

Prior to Beginning

When opposed to silky, straight hair, wavy and curly hair has more texture and grip to hold the braid in place.

Silky hair will get grip from the use of a volumizing powder, making it simpler to braid.

A texture/micro crimping iron can be used to give the hair traction. The crimp effect, though, which you might not want to see, is the drawback.

For braiding, hair that is one or two days old has more grip than newly washed hair.

If set with hairspray and shielded with a silk scarf while you sleep, tighter braids may last two to three days on straight hair.

On natural hair, braiding is utilized to create protective styles that can last up to 12 weeks.

THE DIFFERENT TYPES OF BRAIDS
PONYTAILS AND BUNS

✳ MILKMAID BRAID

A Milkmaid Braid is a classic and charming hairstyle that can be created with medium to long hair. It involves two braids wrapped around the head like a crown. Here's a step-by-step guide on how to make a Milkmaid Braid:

✻ WHAT YOU'LL NEED:

Hairbrush or comb
Hair ties or clear elastics
Bobby pins
Hairspray (optional)

STEPS:

○ Start with clean, dry hair: Ensure your hair is clean and dry before starting the braiding process. If your hair is too slippery, you can add some texture by lightly spritzing it with a texturizing spray or using dry shampoo.

○ Part your hair: Part your hair down the middle to create two equal sections. Use a comb or your fingers to make a straight part.

○ Create two regular braids: On one side of your head, take a small section of hair near your forehead and begin braiding it. Braid this section all the way to the end and secure it with a small hair tie or clear elastic. Repeat the same process on the other side.

○ Loosen the braids: Gently pull on the edges of each braid to loosen them up. This will make the braids appear thicker and more voluminous.

○ Wrap one braid across your head: Take one of the braids and drape it across the top of your head, positioning it just above your forehead like a headband. Use bobby pins to secure it in place. Make sure the pins are hidden under the braid.

○ Wrap the other braid across your head: Take the second braid and do the same thing on the opposite side, bringing it over the top of your head and securing it with bobby pins. It should meet the first braid at the back of your head.

○ Tuck the ends: If the ends of your braids are long, you can tuck them under the opposite braid and secure them with bobby pins to create a seamless look.

○ Adjust and secure: Check to make sure both braids are secure and evenly positioned. Use additional bobby pins if needed.

○ Finish with hairspray: If desired, you can lightly spritz your Milkmaid Braid with hairspray to hold it in place and prevent any flyaways.

○ Optional embellishments: You can accessorize your Milkmaid Braid with decorative pins, flowers, or ribbons for a more personalized and stylish look.

✱ LADDER BRAID WITH BUN

Creating a ladder braid with a bun is a beautiful and intricate hairstyle. The ladder braid adds an interesting element to the bun, making it perfect for special occasions. Here's a step-by-step guide on how to achieve this look:

✱ WHAT YOU'LL NEED:

Hairbrush or comb
Hair ties or clear elastics
Bobby pins
Hairspray (optional)
Hair donut or bun maker (optional)

STEPS:

○ Prepare your hair: Start with clean, dry hair. If you have straight hair, you might want to add some texture with a curling iron or some texturizing spray to give your hair more grip.

○ Create a ponytail: Gather all your hair at the back and secure it into a low ponytail with a hair tie. You can decide how low or high you want the bun to be, but a low bun works well for this style.

○ Divide the ponytail: Split the ponytail into two equal sections. You will be creating the ladder braid with these two sections.

CREATE THE LADDER BRAID:

○ Take a small section of hair from the right side and cross it over the top of the right section.

○ Then, take a small section from the left side and cross it over the top of the left section.

○ Continue this process, alternating sides, to create the ladder braid. You will see the ladder-like pattern forming as you go down the ponytail.

○ Secure the end of the braid with a small hair tie or clear elastic.

○ Pancake the braid: Gently pull on the edges of the ladder braid to make it appear wider and more voluminous. This will give it a more prominent look.

CREATE THE BUN:

○ Now, take the ladder braid and wrap it around the base of the ponytail, forming a bun. You can use a hair donut or bun maker for added volume and a neater bun, or you can simply twist and coil the braid to form the bun.

○ Secure the bun in place using bobby pins. Make sure it's well-anchored to your head.

○ Tuck and secure: If there are any loose ends from the ladder braid, tuck them under the bun and secure them with bobby pins to hide them.

○ Final touches: Gently tug on the ladder braid again to adjust the bun's appearance and make sure the ladder pattern is visible.

Optional hairspray: If desired, you can use a light-hold hairspray to set the style and prevent any flyaways.

Accessories (optional): You can add decorative hairpins, flowers, or other accessories to enhance the look of your ladder braid bun.

✳ LACE BRAID

A lace braid is a beautiful and delicate type of braiding technique that creates the appearance of a braid that seems to sit on top of your hair like a lace ribbon. It's a versatile style that can be used in various hairstyles. Here's how to create a basic lace braid:

✳ WHAT YOU'LL NEED:

Hairbrush or comb
Hair ties or clear elastics
Bobby pins (optional)
Hairspray (optional)

STEPS:

○ Prepare your hair: Start with clean, dry hair. Brush or comb your hair to remove any tangles and make it easier to work with.

○ Part your hair: Decide where you want to create the lace braid. You can do a lace braid along your hairline, on the side, or as part of a more complex hairstyle. Create a part in your hair accordingly.

BEGIN THE BRAID:

For this example, let's assume you're creating a lace braid along your hairline. Gather a small section of hair near the parting.

Divide this section into three smaller sections, just like you would for a regular braid.

Start braiding:

○ Begin a regular three-strand braid by crossing the right section over the middle section.

○ Then, cross the left section over the middle section.

○ This is the starting point of your lace braid.

Add hair to the braid:

○ Unlike a regular braid, where you simply cross the sections over each other, with a lace braid, you add hair only to one side.

○ To do this, as you cross the right section over the middle, pick up a small section of hair from the right side of your head and add it to the right section of the braid.

○ Now, cross the left section over the middle as usual, without adding any new hair.

○ Repeat the process:

○ Continue the braid by adding small sections of hair from the right side of your head to the right section of the braid while crossing it over the middle.

○ Keep the left section of the braid crossing over the middle without adding any new hair.

Continue braiding:

○ Repeat steps 5 and 6 until you've reached the desired length of your lace braid.

○ Secure the end: Once you've added all the hair you want to include in the braid, continue with a regular three-strand braid for a few more stitches. Then, secure the end with a small hair tie or clear elastic.

○ Adjust the braid (optional): Gently tug on the edges of the braid to loosen it and make it appear wider and more delicate, which is the characteristic of a lace braid.

○ Finish (optional): You can use bobby pins to secure the end of the braid against your head, especially if you're creating a lace braid as part of a larger hairstyle.

Hairspray (optional): If desired, you can use a light-hold hairspray to set the style and prevent any flyaways.

✻ FEATHER BRAID

A feather braid is a unique and eye-catching hairstyle that creates the appearance of a delicate, feathery braid. It's a variation of a regular three-strand braid, and it's perfect for adding a touch of elegance to your hair. Here's how to create a basic feather braid:

✻ WHAT YOU'LL NEED:

Hairbrush or comb
Hair ties or clear elastics
Bobby pins (optional)
Hairspray (optional)

STEPS:

○ Prepare your hair: Start with clean, dry hair. Brush or comb your hair to remove any tangles and make it easier to work with.

○ Part your hair: Decide where you want to create the feather braid. You can do a feather braid along your hairline, on the side, or anywhere you'd like to incorporate this style. Create a part in your hair accordingly.

Begin the braid:

○ For this example, let's assume you're creating a feather braid along your hairline. Gather a small section of hair near the parting.

○ Divide this section into three smaller sections, just like you would for a regular three-strand braid.

Start braiding:

○ Begin a regular three-strand braid by crossing the right section over the middle section.

○ Then, cross the left section over the middle section.

○ This is the starting point of your feather braid.

Feather the braid:

○ Unlike a traditional three-strand braid, where you keep the sections tight and close to the head, a feather braid involves gently loosening the braid to create a feathery, voluminous look.

○ After crossing the right section over the middle, use your fingers to gently pull on the edges of the right section to create a loose, feathery effect.

○ Then, cross the left section over the middle and repeat the same process, gently pulling on the edges of the left section to make it look soft and feathered.

○ Continue this feathering technique with each section as you braid.

Continue braiding:

○ Keep repeating the feathering technique with each section as you cross them over the middle.

○ Continue braiding until you've reached the desired length of your feather braid.

○ Secure the end: Once you've finished braiding, secure the end with a small hair tie or clear elastic.

○ Adjust the braid (optional): You can gently tug on the edges of the braid to further loosen and feather it, as needed.

○ Finish (optional): Use bobby pins to secure the end of the braid against your head if you want to keep it in place or incorporate it into a larger hairstyle.

Hairspray (optional): If desired, you can use a light-hold hairspray to set the style and prevent any flyaways.

✳ ROPE BRAID

A rope braid, also known as a twist braid or a two-strand twist, is a simple and elegant hairstyle that involves twisting two strands of hair together to create a spiral-like braid. It's easy to do and can be used for various hairstyles. Here's how to create a basic rope braid:

✳ WHAT YOU'LL NEED:

Hairbrush or comb
Hair ties or clear elastics
Bobby pins (optional)
Hairspray (optional)

STEPS:

○ Prepare your hair: Start with clean, dry hair. Brush or comb your hair to remove any tangles and make it easier to work with.

○ Decide where you want the rope braid: You can create a rope braid in different parts of your hair, such as along your hairline, on the side, or as part of a larger hairstyle. Choose your desired location.

○ Divide your hair: Divide the hair in that area into two equal sections. If you want a more polished look, you can use a comb to create a clean part.

Start twisting:

○ Hold one section of hair in each hand.

○ Begin by twisting one section of hair to the right (clockwise) while simultaneously twisting the other section to the left (counterclockwise).

Cross the sections:

○ After twisting both sections in opposite directions, cross the right section over the left section. This will create the first twist in your rope braid.

Continue twisting and crossing:

○ Continue twisting each section individually in the same directions (right and left) before crossing the right section over the left.

○ Keep repeating this process, ensuring you twist each section tightly to create a neat rope braid.

○ Secure the end: Once you've reached the desired length of your rope braid, secure it with a small hair tie or clear elastic.

○ Adjust the braid (optional): Gently tug on the edges of the rope braid to make it appear wider and more textured. This can give it a more casual and bohemian look.

○ Finish (optional): Use bobby pins to secure the end of the rope braid if you want to keep it in place or incorporate it into a larger hairstyle.

○ Hairspray (optional): If desired, you can use a light-hold hairspray to set the style and prevent any flyaways.

✳ HALO BRAID

Halo braids are also wrapped around the head in a similar manner to crown braids. Halo braids, on the other hand, use the Dutch manner of braiding, which differs slightly from the French technique. The side pieces of the braid cross the main section in French and traditional braided hairstyles. The side parts of the Dutch braid are tucked under the main section. This prevents the braid from blending in with the hair and causes it to stand out.

✳ WHAT YOU NEED

Hair brush
Hair color elastic tie/bands
Bobby pins

✳ HOW TO STYLE

- ○ Comb your hair and create a side part.

- ○ Take some hair from the deep side of the parting and separate it into three sections.

- ○ Begin weaving a Dutch braid with these sections. Keep adding hair to the side sections with every stitch.

- ○ Follow the curve of your hairline as you weave the braid to create the halo circle.

- ○ Use a hair elastic to tie the braid at the end.

- ○ Wrap the Dutch braid's end around your head to complete the halo and secure it with bobby pins.

✳ SIMPLE 3 STRAND BRAID

The simplest of braids, the three-strand simple braid, is one of the most popular hairstyles for ladies that we have all grown up with. Additionally, it's probably the first hairdo you learned on your own. By experimenting with their sizes and textures, this straightforward braid may be made into an infinite number of different hairstyles.

✳ WHAT YOU NEED

Hairbrush
Hair elastic

✳ HOW TO STYLE

○ Brush out all the knots and tangles in your hair

○ Divide your hair into 3 equal sections.

○ Flip the left section over the middle section.

○ Now, flip the right section over the middle section (that was previously the left section).

○ Keep repeating steps 3 and 4 by alternately flipping the left and right sections of hair over the middle section until you have braided till the end.

○ Secure the ends with a hair elastic.

✳ FRENCH BRAID

Here is yet another traditional braid that is popular all around the world. On a steamy summer day, the French braid is the easiest and sexiest way to keep your hair out of your face. It is also the ideal haircut for both work and school. French braiding may take some practice for you to get the hang of, but once you do, it will only take you less than 3 minutes to execute it flawlessly.

✳ WHAT YOU NEED

Hairbrush
Hair elastic

✳ HOW TO STYLE

○ Brush out all the knots from your hair.

○ Pick up the front section of your hair (from between your temples) and divide it into 3 sections.

○ Simply braid it in a stitch.

○ Second stitch onwards, add a 2 inch section of hair from outside the braid to each of the side strands before flipping it over the middle strand of the braid.

○ Once your French braid has reached the nape of your neck and you've run out of hair to add to it, simply braid the rest of the way down and secure the ends with a hair elastic.

○ You can tug apart and loosen the braid, aka pancaking the braid, to make it look more voluminous.

✳ FISHTAIL BRAID

The fishtail or herringbone braid, maybe the most complex braid, is a favorite when it comes to hairstyles for formal occasions. This fashionable braid is made by meticulously weaving together tiny pieces of hair to produce an effect that resembles the symmetrically arranged scales on a fish's tail.

✳ WHAT YOU NEED

Hairbrush
2 hair elastics

✳ HOW TO STYLE

○ Detangle your hair with the help of a hairbrush.

○ Gather all your hair and tie it into a ponytail.

○ Divide your ponytail into 2 equal sections.

○ Pick up a thin section of hair from the outer side of the left section, flip it over and add it to the inner side of the right section of your ponytail.

○ Now, pick up a thin section of hair from the outer side of the right section, flip it over and add it to the inner side of the left section of your ponytail.

○ Keep repeating steps 4 and 5 alternately until you've fishtail braided till the end of your hair.

○ Secure the ends with a hair elastic.

○ Cut off the hair elastic at the top of your braid to finish off the look.

✳ DUTCH BRAID

Dutch braids are simply French braids turned around. Because of how it rests on top of your hair, this braided style offers some fantastic depth. For a flirty look, the Dutch braid can be worn half up, or it can be bunned for a more professional appearance.

✳ WHAT YOU NEED

Hairbrush
Hair elastic

✳ HOW TO STYLE

○ Brush out all the knots and tangles in your hair.

○ From between your temples, pick up the front section of your hair and divide it into 3 sections.

○ Braid it for one stitch by flipping the side sections under the middle section.

○ In each stitch of braid, start adding hair from outside the braid to the side sections before flipping them under the middle section.

○ Once your Dutch braid has reached the nape of your neck, simply braid the rest of the way down and secure the ends with a hair elastic.

✱ WATERFALL BRAID

Nothing compares to the splendor of a waterfall when it comes to breathtaking hairstyles. It seems just how you would expect it to: like a cascade of hair cascading down the side of your head. Waterfall braids are the ideal hairstyle to wear to a wedding or prom because of how beautiful and feminine they look. The feathered or ladder braid is another option if you're searching for a more intricate and refined variant.

✱ WHAT YOU NEED

Hairbrush
Bobby pins

✱ HOW TO STYLE

○ Brush your hair out to remove all knots and tangles.

○ Part your hair on one side.

○ From the side of your parting with more hair, pick up a 3 inch section of hair from the very front and divide it into 3 sections.

○ The section closest to the top of your head is your top section, then there's the middle section, and the section closest to your ear is the bottom section.

○ Do a simple 3 strand braid for one stitch.

○ Now, leave the bottom section and pick up a new section of hair from right next to it to flip over the middle section. This will create the waterfall effect.

○ Add more hair from the top of your head to the top section before flipping it over the middle section.

○ Keep repeating steps 6 and 7 until your waterfall braid has reached the back of your head.

○ Do a simple braid for 3-4 more stitches before pinning down the braid at the back of your head. Make sure you pin it underneath your hair to hide the bobby pins from view.

✳ FORMAL PONYTAIL AND BUN STYLES

Formal events call for hairstyles that are not only elegant but also sophisticated. In this section, we'll explore how to create refined ponytails and buns that are perfect for special occasions. These styles are versatile and can be customized to match the formality of the event, whether it's a wedding, prom, or a fancy dinner party.

ELEGANT AND SOPHISTICATED PONYTAILS:

1. High Sleek Ponytail:

- ○ Start with well-brushed and straightened hair.

- ○ Gather your hair high on the crown of your head

and secure it with a hair elastic.

○ Wrap a small section of hair around the elastic to conceal it and secure with a bobby pin.

○ Smooth out any bumps or flyaways with a fine-toothed comb.

○ Optional: Add a decorative hairpin or jewel-encrusted clip for a touch of glamour. Or add some curl if the hair is longer

2. High Knotted Ponytail:

○ Begin with a high ponytail secured with a hair elastic.

○ Divide the ponytail into two sections.

○ Tie the two sections into a knot and secure it with another hair elastic.

○ Tug gently on the knot to create volume.

○ Optional: Use a tiara or decorative comb to accentuate the knot.

3. Knot Wrapped Ponytail:

- ○ Create a low ponytail and secure it with an elastic.

- ○ Take two strands of hair from the ponytail and knot it around the elastic to hide it.

- ○ Secure the wrapped strands with bobby pins.

- ○ For added elegance, accessorize with a hairpin featuring pearls or rhinestones.

✱ SOPHISTICATED BUN STYLES:

1. Classic French Twist:

○   Gather your hair to one side and hold it as if creating a low side ponytail.

○   Begin twisting your hair upwards while tucking in the sides.

○   Secure the twist with bobby pins along the way.

○   Optional: Insert a decorative hairpin or comb near the twist's base.

2. Low Bun with Chignon:

- ○ Create a low bun at the nape of your neck.

- ○ Add a chignon by rolling a small section of hair and securing it on top of the bun.

- ○ Ensure a polished look with a bit of hairspray and bobby pins as needed.

- ○ Decorate with a delicate tiara or headband for a regal touch.

3. Braided Bun Updo:

- ○ Braid your hair into a classic three-strand or fishtail braid.

- ○ Coil the braid into a bun at the back of your head and secure with bobby pins.

○ Tug on the braid gently to create a fuller look.

○ Adorn with pearl or crystal hairpins for a touch of sophistication.

4. High Double Sided Buns:

○ Split the hair evenly into two high ponytails and secure with an elastic.

○ Roll the ponytail into tight buns and secure with bobby pins.

○ Ensure a polished look with a bit of hairspray and bobby pins as needed.

○ Decorate with a delicate tiara or headband for a regal touch.

TIPS FOR ADDING ACCESSORIES LIKE PINS AND TIARAS:

C hoose Accessories Wisely: Select accessories that complement your outfit and the formality of the event. Consider the color, style, and size of the accessories.

Placement Matters: Place hairpins, clips, or tiaras strategically to enhance your hairstyle. Pins can secure loose strands or add a decorative element, while tiaras can sit atop buns or updos.

Consider Balance: Ensure that the placement of accessories is balanced and symmetrical to create a harmonious look.

Secure Properly: Use bobby pins or hairpins to secure accessories firmly but comfortably. Make sure they don't cause discomfort during the event.

Practice Ahead of Time: If you plan to wear accessories, practice the hairstyle with them to ensure they stay in place and look just right.

With these elegant and sophisticated ponytail and bun styles, along with the right accessories, you'll be ready to shine at any formal event. These timeless looks are sure to leave a lasting impression, highlighting your grace and style.

GOOD HAIRSTYLES FOR SPORTS AND EXERCISE

Exercise, sports, and fitness are vital to our health and are frequently a part of our daily routines. However, our hair frequently suffers as a result of exertion combined with sweat. Long hair could get in the way as we exercise, cling to our faces, and obstruct our vision. How we wear our hairstyles is an important factor to take into account whether we're running on the treadmill or playing tennis.

Ponytail elastics are a chic way for many ladies to keep their hair in place before going to the gym. There are several other flattering hairstyles for sports and activity besides the ponytail.

Using one of these easy solutions can keep your hair neatly tucked away while working out. The best part is that you may still appear stylish and beautiful while working out with these adorable haircuts.

➢ BUN

There is a valid reason why many dancers choose to have their hair tightly bunned. While they dance, the hair is kept in a bun. This haircut also has a refined, stylish appearance that gives any exercise outfit a little extra panache.

Your hair will stay out of the way as you dance or work out if you wear it in a bun. Either a traditional bun or one of its fashionable modifications can be worn. One preferred style is the braided bun. Your hair should first be braided before being bunned firmly. To keep it in place, add more bobby pins and spray some hairspray.

➢ MESSY TOP KNOT

An elegant variation on the traditional bun is the sloppy top knot. This adorable haircut is easy to make and suits all body types. The top knot is a great go-to look for a laid-back gym day.

By putting your hair up in a high ponytail, you may create the sloppy top knot. After that, fasten it using an elastic. Before wrapping your hair up in a knot, divide it into two portions. With bobby pins or elastics, gather all of the loose ends and cinch them underneath your bun.

➢ SPORTY AND ACTIVE HAIRSTYLES

Ponytails and Buns Designed for Physical Activity

Staying active is an essential part of a healthy lifestyle, and having the right hairstyle can make a significant difference in your comfort and performance. In this section, we'll explore sporty and active hairstyles that are perfect for workouts, sports, or any physical activity. These hairstyles are designed to keep your hair secure and comfortable while you stay active.

✳ SPORTY PONYTAIL STYLES:

1. High and Tight Ponytail:

- ○ Brush your hair thoroughly to remove any knots or tangles.

- ○ Gather your hair high on the crown of your head.

- ○ Secure it with a hair elastic, making sure it's tight to minimize bouncing during exercise.

- ○ For extra security, wrap a small section of hair around the elastic and secure it with a bobby pin.

2. Braid-Wrapped Ponytail:

- ○ Create a high ponytail and secure it with an elastic.

- ○ Braid the ponytail and secure the end with another elastic.

- ○ Wrap the braid around the base of the ponytail to create a chic and secure look.

- ○ Use bobby pins to keep the braid in place.

3. Double Ponytail:

- Divide your hair horizontally into two sections, with the upper section being smaller.

- Secure the upper section into a high ponytail.

- Secure the lower section into another ponytail just below the first one.

- This style helps distribute the weight of your hair and reduces pulling during exercise.

✳ ACTIVE BUN STYLES:

1. High Bun with Hairband:

- Gather your hair into a high ponytail and secure it with a hairband.

- Twist the ponytail and wrap it around the hairband to create a bun.

- Secure the bun with bobby pins.

- This style keeps your hair off your neck and prevents it from interfering with your activities.

2. Braided Bun:

- ○ Create a high ponytail and secure it with an elastic.

- ○ Braid the ponytail and secure the end with another elastic.

- ○ Coil the braid into a bun and secure it with bobby pins.

- ○ The braided bun offers excellent hold and control for active pursuits.

Keeping Hair Secure and Comfortable:

1. Use the Right Hair Accessories:

Choose hair elastics, bands, or scrunchies that provide a secure hold without pulling or damaging your hair.

2. Bobby Pins and Hairpins:

Keep bobby pins or hairpins in your sports bag to quickly secure any loose strands during your activity.

3. Headbands and Sweatbands:

Use headbands or sweatbands to keep sweat away from your face and help secure your hairstyle in place.

4. Pre-Workout Preparation:

Brush and detangle your hair before starting your activity to minimize tangles and discomfort during exercise.

5. Post-Workout Care:

After your workout, gently undo your hairstyle and allow your hair to air dry or blow-dry it on a cool setting to prevent excessive sweating and moisture buildup.

These sporty and active hairstyles will not only keep your hair secure and comfortable but also help you focus on your physical performance without distractions. Whether you're hitting the gym, going for a run, or participating in a team sport, these styles have got you covered.

Your support is important to me!
Great things can start from a small gesture!

Please leave a sincere review to support my work.
This would help to share and find this knowledge more easily to people who are looking for it.

HAIR ACCESSORIES - ENHANCING YOUR HAIRSTYLES WITH CLIPS, RIBBONS, AND BEADS

Using Clips, Ribbons, and Beads to Embellish Braids

Hair accessories are the perfect way to add flair and creativity to your hairstyles, especially when working with braids. In this section, we'll explore how to use clips, ribbons, and beads to embellish your braids, making them stand out and showcasing your unique style.

A hat can be a girl's best friend whether she is sprinting out the door or circling the basketball floor. Put one on and you can keep your hair back and the sun off of your eyes. Similarly, headbands and bandanas are great for keeping hair off of your face and eyes.

These hair accessories come in a variety of sizes and hues. The headgear is not only practical, but also fashionable. The headbands, bandanas, and caps may all be coordinated in color to go with your training attire.

EMBELLISHING BRAIDS WITH HAIR CLIPS:

1. Snap Clips:

Snap clips are versatile and easy to use. You can attach them to your braids at regular intervals for a fun and playful look.

2. Decorative Barrettes:

Barrettes come in various shapes and designs. Use them to secure the ends of your braids or as an accent piece along the braid's length.

3. Bobby Pins with Charms:

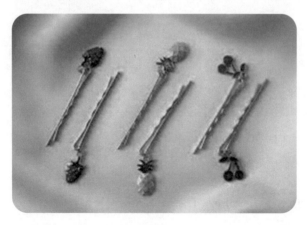

Attach small charms or beads to bobby pins and insert them into your braids for a personalized touch.

✳ USING RIBBONS TO ELEVATE YOUR BRAIDS:

1. RIBBON-WRAPPED BRAIDS:

Choose a ribbon that complements your outfit and the occasion.

Begin wrapping the ribbon around the base of your braid and secure it with a knot.

As you braid your hair, continue incorporating the ribbon by crossing it over each section before you braid it.

Tie the ribbon securely at the end of the braid.

2. RIBBON HEADBANDS:

Turn a ribbon into a headband by tying it around your head and securing it with a bow at the nape of your neck. Let the ends hang down or tuck them into your hairstyle for a sleek look.

✳ ADDING BEADS FOR A BOHO VIBE:

1. BEADED HAIR EXTENSIONS:

Attach small, colorful beads to the ends of your braids using small hair elastics.

These beads add a playful and bohemian touch to your braided hairstyle.

2. BEADED HAIR WRAPS:

Thread beads onto a thin, flexible wire or cord.

Wrap the beaded wire around individual sections of your braids or as a decorative wrap around the entire braid.

CREATIVE WAYS TO INCORPORATE ACCESSORIES INTO HAIRSTYLES:

1. ACCENT BRAIDS:

Create small accent braids (such as fishtail or rope braids) within your main hairstyle.

Use clips, ribbons, or beads to decorate these accent braids, making them the focal point of your look.

2. HALF-UP, HALF-DOWN STYLES:

When styling half-up, half-down hairstyles, use accessories to secure the top section and add interest. Try using decorative clips or ribbons to tie the top section.

3. FLORAL CROWNS:

Create a crown of flowers using artificial or real flowers, securing it in your hair with bobby pins or clips.

4. FESTIVE OCCASIONS:

Match your hair accessories to the theme of special events, like weddings or holidays. For example, opt for pearl accessories for a wedding or red and green ribbon for Christmas.

5. THEMED PARTIES:

Get creative with accessories for themed parties or costume events. Use feathers, glitter, or themed pins to enhance your hairstyle.

Hair accessories offer endless possibilities for expressing your style and adding a personal touch to your hairstyles. Experiment with different combinations of clips, ribbons, and beads to create unique and eye-catching looks that suit your mood and the occasion. Remember, your hair is your canvas, and these accessories are your artistic tools!

HAIR DYEING AS A FORM OF SELF EXPRESSION

A new color is required for the new year! Old is simply monotonous and routine; it's time to liven things up with something novel and unconventional. This is your chance to change the color of your hair, not because we're begging you to, but because you deserve to live in a society that is more accepting and accepting of how people choose to present themselves

The generation of today aspires to create their own identity and separate out from the crowd. They make snap decisions, therefore dyeing your hair can help you control your impulses. These young people's thoughts have a special outlet through their colored hair, and it inspires others to welcome change. You can feel more in control of your thoughts and actions, allowing you to be who you truly are.

WHAT IS A TEMPORARY COLOR? WHAT IS THE DURATION OF IT?

The cortex of the hair are not penetrated by temporary hair color. Instead, it applies color to the hair shaft's outside, which is washed away in one to two shampoos. There is no chemical reaction, but if the hair is porous and damaged, the color can seep in and stain it. Temporary color is perfect to "make do" between sessions with your hairdresser or for last-minute touch-ups before a large party.

Temporary Hair Color - Adding Vibrant Accents to Your Braids

Experimenting with Temporary Hair Color Products

Temporary hair color allows you to explore your creativity and temporarily transform your hair without making a long-term commitment. In this section, we'll delve into the exciting world of temporary hair color products and how you can use them to add vibrant accents to your braids.

TYPES OF TEMPORARY HAIR COLOR PRODUCTS:

1. Hair Chalk:

Hair chalk is a popular choice for temporary color. It's easy to apply and comes in various vibrant shades.

To use hair chalk, dampen the section of hair you want to color, rub the chalk onto the hair, and seal the color with heat or hair spray.

2. Temporary Hair Spray:

Temporary hair spray offers a wide range of colors and allows you to create bold, colorful accents in seconds.

Simply spray the color onto your braids, and it will wash out with your next shampoo.

3. Colored Hair Gels or Waxes:

These products provide a strong hold along with temporary color.

Apply them to your braids like you would regular gel or wax, and enjoy colorful and structured braids.

4. Hair Mascara or Paint:

Hair mascara or paint is a precise way to add color to your braids.

Brush the color onto specific sections or strands for a more controlled and detailed result.

5. Temporary Hair Dye Pens:

These pens resemble markers and are perfect for adding intricate designs or precise accents to your braids.

TIPS FOR USING TEMPORARY HAIR COLOR:

What information should beginners have before coloring their hair?

To be sure you are not experiencing an allergic reaction, it is always advisable to undergo a patch test. To do this, pick a discrete location and a tiny patch of skin the size of a penny, such as the fold of skin inside your elbow or behind your ear. After cleaning it with soap and water, dry it with a fresh towel. Apply a tiny layer of the dye of your choice to the test area, let it dry, and then leave it alone for 24 hours. Look for any indications of inflammation there.

Under no circumstances should the product be used if there is a negative reaction. Strand tests are a fantastic approach to guarantee that you receive the outcomes you want!

Before attempting to color a large portion of freshly shampooed and dried hair, color a small discrete section first. To prevent skin from getting stained around your hairline, apply petroleum jelly or a heavy conditioner. Wear latex gloves. Prevent the color from staining your clothes and anything else.

Apply the conditioner to the portions you want to remain undisturbed if you only want the color in a specific spot. In doing so, it will serve as a "color blocker" and keep the surrounding region "color free." If using more than one color, use foil to divide each part. Use a double-sided tint brush to apply color, working from the roots outward, section by section. Put a plastic cap on top, and wait 30 minutes. Rinse until almost clear, avoiding the face and body, using cool or cold water to remove the color.

WHAT ARE THE BEST WAYS TO CARE FOR COLORED HAIR?

After coloring the hair once, conditioning is not necessary. However, rinsing the hair immediately after coloring with a solution made of equal parts white vinegar and water can help to keep the color vibrant longer. After properly rinsing, comb through and let it sit for a few minutes. The pH level of the hair is increased as a result, improving color performance. After dyeing your hair, we advise waiting about a week before shampooing or conditioning. Use a moderate or gentle washing shampoo that is free of sulphates, oils, and clarifiers, or use dry shampoo.

HOW TO MAINTAIN BRAIDS, ACCORDING TO A NATURAL HAIR EXPERT

Why wouldn't you love braids? Protective hairstyles never go out of style, from box braids to Fulani braids. Although they are expensive to maintain and take a lot of time, money, and patience (so much patience), the results are always worthwhile. We consulted a natural hair specialist to understand how to manage our braids and keep them looking as good as the day we had them done in order to keep the style preserved, moisturized, and long-lasting.

✻ HYDRATE YOUR SCALP

According to Kendall Dorsey, a celebrity hairstylist and the brand ambassador for Dark & Lovely, "maintaining the health of your scalp and adding moisture to your hair is the most important thing to consider when wearing a protective style." Your scalp will be more exposed than usual for the majority of styles (such box braids and cornrows). It may be more prone to dryness, irritability, and/or flakiness as a result. You must frequently hydrate your scalp and hair in order to prevent this.

✱ FREQUENT BRAID WASHING

The idea that you shouldn't wash your hair if you have braids is a common misconception. To be clear, that is wholly untrue. You can wash your braids without fear of destroying the style, of course. In fact, it's imperative that you regularly clean your braids and scalp to prevent any product accumulation, dryness, or irritation.

✱ DO NOT WEAR TIGHT HAIRSTYLES.

The greatest quality of braids is their adaptability. You can be wearing them down one moment and then pulling them up in a ponytail the next. However, you should be mindful about how frequently you wear these fashionable haircuts. Your braids are more likely to frizz, break, and weaken along the roots and edges if you wear them in tight styles all the time, such as high ponytails, buns, dutch braids, etc. Now, we're not saying you should stop wearing these fashions altogether; rather, limit your use of them to twice weekly to prevent any tearing or tugging. Your scalp will appreciate it later, we promise.

✱ RESTYLE YOUR HAIRLINE BRAIDS AND EDGES.

Using a gentle wash and some coconut oil to keep the region moisturized, you can think about redoing your edges every four weeks if you have the time (and patience). Along with tidying up your baby hairs, you might want to (depending on the style you're wearing) also think about retouching the braids that run along your hairline. This will maintain the look's freshness and give the impression that you completely redone it.

✱ KEEP YOUR BRAIDS COVERED AT NIGHT.

We could go on and on about the benefits of always covering your hair at night. Simply said, unprotected hair loses moisture and gloss and is more prone to frizz. Dorsey advises covering your hair in a silk or satin scarves (or bonnet) to prevent friction and dryness while you sleep. Use a silk pillowcase as well for additional protection (and in case you wake up with your scarf on the other side of the room).

✱ AVOID KEEPING YOUR BRAIDS IN PLACE TOO LONG.

You can wear braids for a very long time, yes. But you shouldn't leave them on for too long. Dorsey advises limiting the duration of protective styles to four to six weeks. Why? Your hair needs a break, just like you book PTO to take a break from work. Your hair will be more prone to breakage, knots, and tangles the longer you leave your braids in. They are protective styles, indeed, but only in the short term.

Are your braids an absolute necessity? Take a vacation (for about a week) and rework them in a whole fresh way. Braids shouldn't damage your natural hair; rather, they should be a pleasant method to flaunt a fresh look.

AUTHORS ACKNOWLEDGEMENT

Dear Readers,

As we reach the end of this journey together, I want to extend my sincere gratitude to each and every one of you who has embarked on this exploration of BRAIDS, PONYTAILS & BUNS FOR YOUNG GIRLS with me. Writing this book has been a fun journey, driven by a passion to ensure young girls all over the world feel confident with this appearance and have high self asteem.

Throughout these pages, we've provided lots of cool ways to style your young daughters hair including accessories that can provide additional glamour for those special party days. My hope has always been to provide you with valuable information, spark your curiosity, and inspire you to take action.

Remember that the final chapter of this book is just the beginning of your journey with ALL THINGS HAIR. Continue to ask questions, seek knowledge, and explore the ever-evolving landscape of this topic.

Thank you for joining me on this fun filled adventure. Your time and attention are precious, and I am humbled by your choice to spend them with this book. I hope the knowledge and insights you've gained here serve you well in your own pursuits.

I look forward to hearing about your experiences, thoughts, and actions inspired by this book. Please feel free to connect with me via email info@bookwormltd.co.nz as I value the opportunity to continue our dialogue.

In closing, may your journey of discovery and lifelong learning be as rewarding as the one we've shared in these pages. Until we meet again in the world of ideas and knowledge.

With heartfelt appreciation,

Shelby Welborn

Your support is important to me!
Great things can start from a small gesture!

**Please leave a sincere review to support my work.
This would help to share and find this knowledge more easily to
people who are looking for it.**

Made in United States
Troutdale, OR
07/12/2024